PECULIAR PLANTS

Anita Ganeri

www.raintreepublishers.co.uk
Visit our website to find out more information about Raintree books.

To order:
☎ Phone 0845 6044371
🖷 Fax +44 (0) 1865 312263
🖳 Email myorders@raintreepublishers.co.uk

Customers from outside the UK please telephone +44 1865 312262

Raintree is an imprint of Capstone Global Library Limited, a company incorporated in England and Wales having its registered office at 7 Pilgrim Street, London, EC4V 6LB – Registered company number: 6695582

Edited by Dan Nunn, Rebecca Rissman, and Catherine Veitch
Designed by Cynthia Della-Rovere
Picture research by Tracy Cummins
Production by Alison Parsons
Originated by Capstone Global Library
Printed and bound in China by CTPS

ISBN 978 1 406 23790 0
16 15 14 13 12
10 9 8 7 6 5 4 3 2 1

British Library Cataloguing in Publication Data
Ganeri, Anita
Peculiar plants. -- (Extreme nature)
581.4-dc22
A full catalogue record for this book is available from the British Library.

Acknowledgements
We would like to thank the following for permission to reproduce photographs: Corbis pp. 4 (© Michael DeFreitas/Robert Harding World Imager), 7 (© Frans Lanting), 11 (© Henry Lehn/Visuals Unlimited), 26 (© Mauricio Handler/National Geographic Society); Getty Images pp. 5 (Martin Harvey), 9 (Altrendo Panoramic), 13 (Coke Whitworth), 16 (David C Tomlinson), 24 (Roger de la Harpe), 25 (China Photos/Stringer); National Geographic Stock p. 6 (FRANS LANTING), 19 (KONRAD WOTHE/ MINDEN PICTURES), 22 (MICHAEL & PATRICIA FOGDEN/MINDEN PICTURES); Photolibrary pp. 10 (Malcolm Schuyl/FLPA), 15 (Nick Garbutt), 17 (HSchweiger Hschweiger), 18 (Jean-Philippe Delobelle); Shutterstock pp. 8 (© Jorg Hackemann), 12 (© a9photo), 14 (© Calvin Chan), 20 (© hunta), 21 (© gary yim), 23 (© Pichugin Dmitry), 27 (© Heather A. Craig).

Cover photograph of a rafflesia reproduced with permission of Getty Images (Renaud Visage).

Every effort has been made to contact copyright holders of material reproduced in this book. Any omissions will be rectified in subsequent printings if notice is given to the publisher.

Some words are shown in bold, **like this**. You can find out what they mean by looking in the glossary.

Contents

What are peculiar plants?

Did you know that some trees grow taller than skyscrapers? Or that some plants eat mice? Peculiar plants grow all over the world. Some plants are record-breakers. Others have special **features** to help them live in **hostile**, or unfriendly, **habitats**.

mangrove tree

Stone plants look like stones to hide from hungry animals.

Freaky flower

The rafflesia flower grows in the **rainforest** in south-east Asia. It is the world's biggest flower and smells of rotten meat.

rafflesia bud

DID YOU KNOW?
The rafflesia can grow up to one metre across. That's about as wide as your outstretched arms.

Towering tree

A giant sequoia tree, nicknamed the "General Sherman" tree, grows in California, USA. It is as tall as 15 houses and is the biggest tree on Earth.

GENERAL SHERMAN

DID YOU KNOW?

The "General Sherman" contains enough wood to make billions of matchsticks.

Strangler fig

The strangler fig grows in the **rainforest**. Its seed **sprouts** high up on the branch of another tree. Then the roots grow down towards the ground and wrap tightly around the tree. The roots suck up the tree's water supply and the tree dies.

DID YOU KNOW?
The strangler fig was given its name because it strangles other plants to death.

Meat-eating plants

The Venus flytrap plant eats insects in a nasty way. The insect touches some hairs on the plant. This makes the leaf snap shut, trapping the insect. Then the plant makes special juices that turn the insect's body into liquid for the plant to soak up.

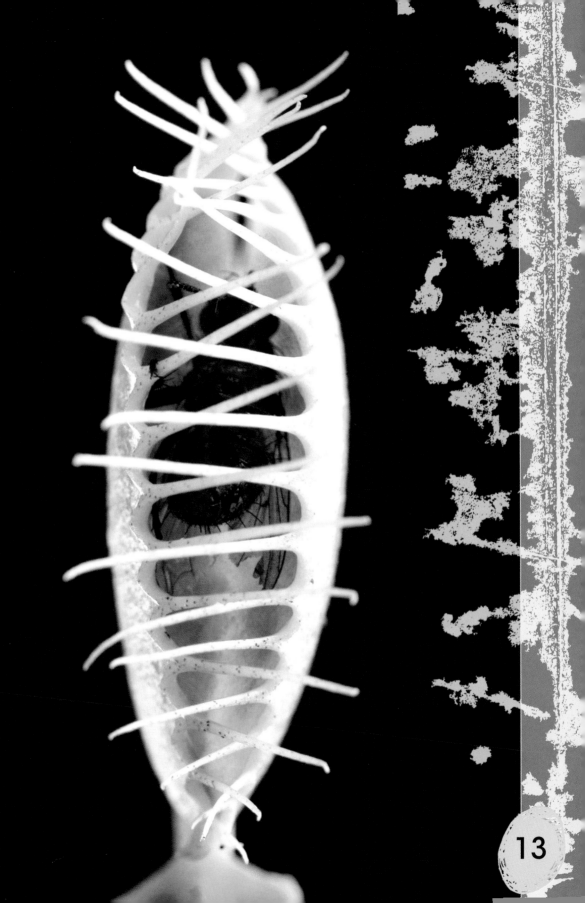

Pitcher plants have strange, jug-shaped leaves. Insects land on the leaves, looking for **nectar** to drink. But they slide down into the "jug" and drown in the pool of water inside. Then the plant **digests** them.

DID YOU KNOW?
The biggest pitcher plant, the Rajah, catches the poo of small animals such as rats and mice.

Prickly plants

Giant saguaro cacti grow in the deserts of the United States and Mexico. They can weigh 10 tonnes. That's as heavy as six large cars!

The cacti store water in their thick stems to use when there is a **drought**.

Bulging baobab

A baobab tree has branches that stick up into the air and look like upside-down roots. They store water in their trunks, which bulge as they fill up.

DID YOU KNOW?
There is a **legend** that anyone who picks a baobab flower will be eaten by a lion.

Baobabs mostly grow on the island of Madagascar, off the **coast** of Africa.

Out in the cold

High up on a mountain, it is windy and cold. Mountain plants have special ways to keep warm. The flowers and leaves of edelweiss are covered in furry white hairs to keep it warm.

The edelweiss is a tiny plant that grows in the Alps mountains.

Snow **algae** from icy Antarctica have a chemical inside them that stops their bodies from freezing. This algae colours the snow red.

Weird welwitschia

The welwitschia grows in the Namib Desert in Namibia, in Africa. The leaves collect **dew**, which the plant needs to stay alive. The plant has only two leaves. But the leaves get torn to pieces by the wind.

DID YOU KNOW?
The leaves of the welwitschia plant can grow almost as long as a bus.

Giant water lily

Giant water lily leaves float on the Amazon River in South America. Each leaf can grow more than 2 metres wide (the size of a small garden pond).

DID YOU KNOW?
Water lily leaves float because they have spaces filled with air inside them.

Giant water lily leaves are very strong. People can sit on one without sinking!

Super-sized seaweed

Huge seaweed forests grow along the **coast** of California in the United States. This seaweed is called giant kelp. It has ribbon-like stems that can grow over 50 metres long. That is about as long as two swimming pools!

DID YOU KNOW?
A giant kelp stem can grow as tall as an adult person in just four days.

Sea otters live among the stems of giant kelp.

Quiz: What am I?

Read the clues, then try to work out "What am I?". Find the answers at the bottom of page 29. But guess first!

1) I have orange-brown petals.
I smell of rotten meat.
I can grow up to one metre across.
What am I?

2) I grow in the **rainforest**.
I strangle other trees.
I **sprout** on a tree branch.
What am I?

3) I have hairy leaves.
I eat insects.
My name is also a planet.
What am I?

4) I float on a river.
I can be as big as a pond.
I am strong enough to sit on.
What am I?

5) I grow in the desert.
My leaves are as
long as a bus.
I drink **dew**.
What am I?

Glossary

algae plants that often live in water. Seaweed is a type of algae.

coast edge of the land that borders the sea

dew drops of water that form at night on plants and other surfaces

digest change food so that it can be taken into the body

drought time of very dry weather when there is very little or no rain

feature special body part, pattern, or kind of behaviour

habitat place where a plant or an animal lives

hostile difficult to live in; not very friendly or welcoming

legend ancient story that may or may not be true

nectar sweet syrup found deep inside flowers

rainforest forest that is warm and wet all year round

sprout spread out shoots

Find out more

Books

Plants! (*Time for Kids Science Scoops*), Brenda Iasevoli (Harper Trophy, 2006)

The Deadliest Plants on Earth (*The World's Deadliest*), Connie Colwell Miller (Raintree, 2011)

Venus Flytraps, Bladderworts and Other Wild and Amazing Plants (National Geographic Science Chapters series), Monica Halpern (National Geographic Society, 2006)

Websites

www.edenproject.com

This is the website of the Eden Project in Cornwall. The Eden Project has plants from around the world, including a rainforest you can walk through.

www.kew.org

This is the website of the Royal Botanic Gardens at Kew, London, which has a huge collection of peculiar plants from around the world.

Index

Many female pandas have been made pregnant by artificial insemination. Pandas can be very aggressive to each other and there is a risk that either animal could be injured. This risk is avoided by using AI.

Surrogate mothers

Sometimes, there are so few females in the breeding programme that it is necessary to use a **surrogate** mother. This is usually a female of a closely related species. The embryo is implanted into the uterus of the surrogate, where it develops as normal. This method means that many more young can be produced, speeding up the breeding programme. For example, in 2001, a domestic sheep gave birth to a Mouflon lamb, a rare wild sheep.

The first endangered species to be born to a surrogate mother was an African wildcat called Jazz (left in the photo), in 1999. Following research by Dr Betsy Dresser and her team at the Audubon Center for Research of Endangered Species, they successfully implanted the embryo of an African wildcat into the uterus of a tabby cat.

A frozen zoo

It is relatively easy to store seeds for the future (see pages 26–27), but this is not easy with animal tissue. However, with animals becoming extinct every day, it is becoming increasingly urgent to collect and store their DNA in so-called frozen zoos.

Animal cells can be frozen and then stored for long periods of time. If they have been frozen correctly, they resume their normal functions when thawed. First, an anti-freeze is added to the cells to stop ice crystals from forming, and then the cells are stored in tanks of liquid nitrogen at -196 °C. The use of liquid nitrogen avoids the need for an electricity supply to maintain the temperature, and the cells can be transported safely in the tanks.

This method was first used to store sperm from bulls during the 1940s. Today, a wide range of cell and tissue samples can be stored. However, eggs are difficult to store, so they are collected from female animals, fertilized, and then stored as embryos.

↑ Samples of sperm are stored at extremely low temperatures, so protective clothing has to be worn when removing samples from the storage canisters.

Collecting samples

In 1975, Kurt Benirschke, a researcher at The Centre for Reproduction of Endangered Species at San Diego Zoo in the United States, started a project that involved collecting and freezing cells from different rare animals. The aim was to compare the similarities between the different species. Today, there are samples from about 800 species, mostly mammals, in this frozen zoo.

Similar frozen collections are being set up at other research centres. The genetic material can be used for research but it also represents a safety net should an animal become extinct. For example, there are just 30 Gobi bears (a sub-species of the brown bear) left in the wild, and none in zoos. Biologists fitted tracking collars to some of the bears and at the same time they took cell samples. These cells have been grown in the laboratory and stored. The genetic material could be used in the future to produce Gobi bear embryos using cloning techniques (see pages 46–47).

Cryo-chick

The Mississippi sandhill crane is an endangered bird species, of which just 100 remain in the United States. As part of a captive breeding programme, researchers are keen to make sure that the birds do not become too inbred. In 2007, biologists at the Audubon Center for Research of Endangered Species used frozen sperm to fertilize an egg and a chick hatched successfully (left). This is one of several cryo-chicks produced using frozen sperm (cryo means cold). These advances make it possible for breeding centres to swap frozen sperm to maintain the genetic diversity of their animals. The cryo-chick will be raised with the others bred by normal means at the Centre and then it will be released into the wild at the Mississippi Sandhill Crane National Refuge.

Cloning

Sourcing egg cells for animal reproduction can be problematic. Eggs cannot be stored, so they need to be collected fresh. This requires a surgical operation, which can be too risky for many endangered animals, especially species such as the giant panda. One alternative is cloning.

What is a clone?

A **clone** is a genetic copy of another individual. Clones can be produced naturally; for example identical twins are clones. Some insects make clones of themselves by asexual reproduction (reproduction that involves only one individual). When this happens, all the offspring are genetically identical to the parent.

Scientists at Advanced Cell Technology in the United States attempted to clone a gaur, a rare species of wild ox. Eventually, a calf called Noah was born, but he died two days later.

 THE SCIENCE YOU LEARN: CLONES AND EMBRYOS

How can an animal be cloned? First, a nucleus is taken from a cell of the animal to be cloned – the donor. Next, an egg cell is taken from another animal, either of the same species or from a closely related species, and the nucleus removed. The nucleus from the donor is slipped into the empty egg cell. The egg receives a small electric shock, which causes it to start to divide and grow into an embryo. The embryo is then placed into the uterus of a surrogate animal and allowed to develop naturally.

It sounds easy, but it takes many years and many attempts before a cloned animal is born. Chinese biologists have recently produced a cloned embryo of a giant panda, using an egg cell from a white rabbit. Now the biologists are looking for a suitable surrogate for the cloned panda embryos.

Clones can also be produced artificially in the laboratory. The best known clone is probably Dolly the sheep, who was born in 1996. She was genetically identical to her mother. Some biologists want to reproduce endangered species using cloning.

Cloning – is it right?

There are lots of arguments for and against cloning. Cloning is still in the experimental stage and often many hundreds of eggs are used before success is achieved. Many clones have been born with abnormalities which cause them to die, while the clones that survive have a shorter than average lifespan. Pets are being cloned and some people think that it is only a matter of time before the first human clones are created. However, because of the risks involved, human cloning research is banned or tightly controlled in most countries.

The thylacine or Tasmanian tiger was a carnivorous marsupial that once roamed Australia and New Guinea. It became extinct on the Australian mainland 2,000 years ago but survived on Tasmania until 1930 when the last one was shot.

CUTTING EDGE: BACK FROM THE DEAD

Some scientists claim it will be possible to extract DNA from the remains of recently extinct animals, such as the thylacine or quagga, and recreate them in the laboratory. But even if this could be achieved, there would still be problems. For example, the genetic material may come from just one animal, so all the recreations would be male or female and there would be no genetic diversity. Also, there may be no suitable habitat for the cloned animals. The likelihood is that they would spend their lives in a zoo.

Threatened species case studies

There are many threatened species around the world. Here are a few selected case studies.

Golden lion tamarin

Golden lion tamarin (*Leontopithecus rosalia*) is an endangered species of primate that is found in a small area of tropical rainforest in Brazil. Widespread deforestation of its Atlantic rainforest habitat resulted in the wild population falling to just 200 in 1971. With extinction very likely, various conservation agencies set up The Golden Tamarin Conservation Programme. This involved reintroducing captive-born tamarins back into the wild and moving small populations to large forest reserves, where they could be better protected. This has proved to be successful and, in 2001, the population reached 1,000 in the wild and 500 in zoos. It is now classed as "endangered", rather than "critically endangered". However, the conservation work continues and there are plans to establish new protected areas.

Great bustards

The great bustard (*Otis tarda*) is a large ground bird, about the size of a turkey, which is found on grasslands such as the steppes of Russia and the arable fields of Europe. The last great bustards in Britain were shot during the 1840s. This removed a key animal from the food web of the downlands and farmland of southern England. A similar fate befell the great bustard in other parts of Europe. However, a modest population of great bustards remained in Russia and, since 2004, young birds from Russia have been released into pens on the grasslands of Salisbury Plain in Britain. The birds have settled in well and it is hoped that they will start breeding by 2009. The other remaining stronghold of the great bustard is Spain, where there are an estimated 23,000 birds living in the central plains.

Ne-ne

The Ne-ne, or Hawaiian goose (*Branta sandvicensis*), is a native species of bird in Hawaii. Predation from introduced animals such as dogs and rats, together with habitat loss, caused the population of the Ne-ne to decrease to just 30 individuals in 1952. A captive breeding programme was set up by Sir Peter Scott at the Wildfowl and Wetlands Trust in the United Kingdom. The Ne-ne adapted well to captivity and numbers increased. Captive-bred birds were reintroduced to Hawaii and populations have revived. The species is now classed as "vulnerable".

Père David's deer

Père David's deer (*Elaphurus davidianus*) is a critically endangered species of deer that is found only in China. A priest, Father Armand David came across a herd of the deer when he was working in China during the nineteenth century. The herd was owned by the Chinese Emperor. A few specimens were taken to Britain, where they bred successfully in captivity on the Duke of Bedford's estate, Woburn Abbey. The deer have since died out in China, so conservationists gathered the remaining animals and bred from them. During the 1980s, some deer were reintroduced into two protected areas in China. By 2005 there were an estimated 1,300 deer living in China.

Mallorcan midwife toad

The Mallorcan midwife toad (*Alytes muletensis*), a type of amphibian, is unusual because the males carry the strings of eggs wrapped around their back legs. This protects the eggs from predators. This toad was first identified from fossils that were dated at five million years old. Biologists thought that this species had become extinct several thousand years ago. Amazingly, in 1977, midwife toads were discovered living in some inaccessible canyons on the Mediterranean island of Mallorca (Majorca). Only a small population had survived, so some were taken into captivity and bred. The toads have been reintroduced and the numbers in the wild have increased. However, like many other amphibians, they are still threatened by climate change and disease.

Bumblebee bat

The bumblebee bat (*Craseonycteris thonglongyai*) is the world's smallest mammal. It weighs less that 2 g (0.07 oz), and is about the size of a bumblebee, hence its name. It is found in caves in Thailand and Myanmar. In the past, the bats were collected and sold as tourist souvenirs. Today, the main threats are the burning of forests near the bats' caves and disturbance from too many tourists visiting the caves. The bat is protected in Thailand, where a reserve has been established to help its conservation. However, more action is needed to protect the caves from people. Also, more surveys need to be carried out in Myanmar, to establish the extent of the problem and help inform solutions that can protect the bats.

Facts and figures

Threatened species timeline

1872   The Yellowstone National Park is created in the western United States.

1886   The Audubon Society is established in the United States.

1889   The Royal Society for the Protection of Birds (RSPB) is established in the United Kingdom.

1892   The Sierra Club is established in the United States.

1895   Svante August Arrhenius, a Swedish chemist, publishes his theories on the importance of carbon dioxide content of the atmosphere for the climate.

1895   The National Trust is established in the United Kingdom. Its first acquisition is a length of coastline in Wales.

1910   The Audubon Society leads a campaign to boycott hat makers that use feathers from endangered birds.

1949   The first United Nations Conference on the Environment.

1958   The Wolong National Park is established in China to protect the giant panda.

1961   The World Wildlife Fund (WWF) is established.

1962   American biologist, Rachel Carson publishes *Silent Spring*, a book that warns of the threats from the overuse of pesticides.

1970   Establishment of the US EPA (United States Environmental Protection Agency).
The first Earth Day takes place around the world, to inspire awareness of and appreciation for the Earth's environment.

1971   The environmental charity Greenpeace is established.

1972   WWF launches Operation Tiger to conserve the tiger in India.
The first United Nations Environment Conference in Stockholm, Sweden, when the UN Environment Programme headquarters is established in Nairobi, Kenya.

1973   The Convention on International Trade in Endangered Species (CITES) is signed by 80 nations.

1975	The WWF carries out its first campaign to protect tropical rainforests.
1976	Brazilian environmental activist, Chico Mendes leads a campaign to stop logging in the Amazonian rainforest.
1980	The WWF, World Conservation Union, and United Nations Environmental Programme (UNEP) launch their World Conservation Strategy to encourage sustainable development.
1989	The oil tanker *Exxon Valdez* runs aground in Alaska spilling millions of litres of oil.
1990	Earth Day marks its 20th anniversary, with 140 nations taking part. The United Nations Intergovernmental Panel on Climate Change (IPCC) publishes its first report, giving warnings of global warming.
1991	Antarctic Treaty agrees to protect animals and prevent mining and pollution.
2000	The Millennium Seed Bank Project is established in West Sussex, United Kingdom.
2001	Noah, the world's first cloned gaur (an endangered species) is born, but dies of a common disease in newborns two days later.
2006	The WWF launches the Heart of Borneo Campaign, to help conserve tropical rainforests.
2007	The Zoological Society of London launches EDGE (Evolutionarily Distinct and Globally Endangered), a conservation programme aimed at protecting some of the world's most bizarre animals that are often overlooked by conservationists.

Find out more

Books

Adams, Douglas and Mark Carwardine. *Last Chance to See* (Pan Books, 1991)

Barraclough, Sue. *Protecting Species and Habitats* (Smart Apple Media, 2006)

Carson, Rachel. *Silent Spring* (Library bound edn., Sagebrush, 1999)

Garbutt, Nick. *100 Animals to See Before They Die* (Bradt Travel Guides, 2007)

Kazlowski, Steven. *The Last Polar Bear* (Mountaineers Books, 2008)

Websites

http://cms.iucn.org
The International Union for Conservation of Nature publishes the Red List – the list of endangered species in the world.

www.toothandclaw.org.uk
Tooth and Claw. Visit this website to learn about predators and their relationship with people, covering emotive topics such as wolf and bear reintroductions in modern Britain.

www.edgeofexistence.org
EDGE is the conservation programme launched by the Zoological Society of London. EDGE stands for Evolutionarily Distinct and Globally Endangered.

www.wwf.org
This website gives information about the World Wildlife Fund's current conservation campaigns.

www.audubon.org
The National Audubon Society website describes the work of the society to promote conservation of natural ecosystems.

Topics to research

- Find out more about reintroducing predators, such as wolves and bears, into modern Britain. A good starting point is the Tooth and Claw website where there are articles on predators and how they could be reintroduced.

- Did you know that some people are paying to have their pets cloned? As technology improves, it may become routine to clone animals. Find out more about this very controversial topic.

Glossary

allele form of gene

biodiversity total number of species living in a particular area

captive breeding keeping animals in order to breed from them

carrying capacity number of individuals that a habitat can support

chromosome structure found in the nucleus, made of DNA and protein

classify put an animal or plant into a group or class of species

clone identical genetic copy of another individual

conservation protection and preservation of habitats, species, or natural resources

consumer animal in the food chain that feeds on either plants or other animals

diversity degree of variation

DNA (deoxyribonucleic acid) molecule that carries the genetic information and makes up chromosomes

dominant allele form of a gene that will always show itself. It masks a recessive allele.

embryo cell formed when an egg is fertilized by a sperm

enzyme type of protein that speeds up a chemical reaction

extinct no longer in existence

food chain very simple representation of the feeding relationships that exist between living things

food web number of food chains in a particular habitat that are linked together

gamete sex cell, such as egg or sperm

gene unit of inheritance that is passed from parent to offspring; a section of DNA that codes for the production of a protein or a small group of proteins

genetic fingerprint visual representation of a person's DNA that looks a bit like a bar code and which can be used for identification purposes

germination process of a seed beginning to grow

gestation period period of pregnancy, from fertilization to birth

habitat place where a plant or animal lives

heathland habitat with thin, sandy soils and low-growing plants, such as heather and gorse

hormone chemical messenger carried around the body in the blood

implantation placing an embryo in the uterus of a female animal

inbreeding mating of closely related individuals

marsupial type of mammal that gives birth to undeveloped young that are placed in a pouch to complete their growth

metamorphosis physical change that occurs in the growth cycle of some creatures

niche role of a species within a community

pollinators insects and animals that transfer pollen (male gametes) from one plant to the ovule (female gamete) of another plant, to enable the sexual reproduction of plants

population total number of individuals of a species living in a particular area

predator animal that hunts and kills other animals for food

producer organism at the bottom of the food chain, such as a plant or bacterium, that can make its own food

recessive allele form of a gene that will only show itself if both alleles are recessive

Red List list of endangered species produced by the International Union for Conservation of Nature

savannah large area of grassland with few trees in southern Africa

speciation formation of a new species

succession sequence of changes that occur from bare ground to woodland

surrogate female animal that gives birth to the baby of another animal

sustainable able to be maintained at the same level

variation differences between individuals

viable capable of germinating and growing into a new plant

Index

Finding Shapes

Squares

Diyan Leake

Raintree

www.raintreepublishers.co.uk

Visit our website to find out more information about **Raintree** books.

To order:
- ☎ Phone 44 (0) 1865 888112
- 📄 Send a fax to 44 (0) 1865 314091
- 💻 Visit the Raintree Bookshop at **www.raintreepublishers.co.uk** to browse our catalogue and order online.

First published in Great Britain by Raintree,
Halley Court, Jordan Hill, Oxford OX2 8EJ,
part of Harcourt Education.
Raintree is a registered trademark of Harcourt
Education Ltd.

Editorial: Diyan Leake
Design: Joanna Hinton-Malivoire
Picture research: Maria Joannou
Production: Chloe Bloom
Originated by Dot Gradations Ltd
Printed and bound in China by
South China Printing Company

ISBN 1 844 21333 1
10 09 08 07 06
10 9 8 7 6 5 4 3 2 1

British Library Cataloguing in Publication Data
Leake, Diyan
516.5
Finding Shapes: Squares
A full catalogue record for this book is available
from the British Library.

Acknowledgements
The publisher would like to thank the following
for permission to reproduce photographs:
Corbis p. **12** (Craig Lovell); Getty Images pp. **5**
(Imagebank/Kaz Mori), **13** (Imagebank/Cyril Isy-
Schwart), 21 (Photodisc), **23** (straight,
Imagebank/Kaz Mori); Harcourt Education Ltd
pp. **6** (Malcom Harris), **7** (Tudor Photography),
8 (Tudor Photography), **9** (Malcolm Harris), **10**
(Malcolm Harris), **11** (Malcolm Harris), **15**
(Malcolm Harris), **16** (Tudor Photography),
17 (Malcolm Harris), **18** (Malcolm Harris), **19**
(Malcolm Harris), **22** (Malcolm Harris), **23**
(cube, Malcolm Harris; edges, Malcolm Harris;
faces, Tudor Photography; solid, Malcolm Harris),
back cover (cube, Malcolm Harris); Rex Features
p. **14** (Dave Penman)

Cover photograph reproduced with the
permission of Corbis

Every effort has been made to contact copyright
holders of any material reproduced in this book.
Any omissions will be rectified in subsequent
printings if notice is given to the publishers.

The author and publisher would like to thank
Patti Barber, specialist in Early Years Education,
University of London Institute of Education, for
her advice and assistance in the preparation of
this book.

The paper used to print this book comes from
sustainable resources.

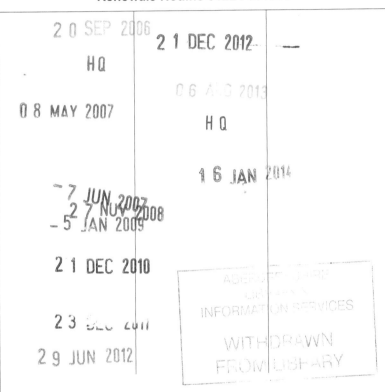
LEAKE, Diyan

Squares

Contents

Some words are shown in bold, **like this**. They are explained in the glossary on page 23.

What is a square?

A square is **flat** shape.

It is a special kind of **rectangle**.

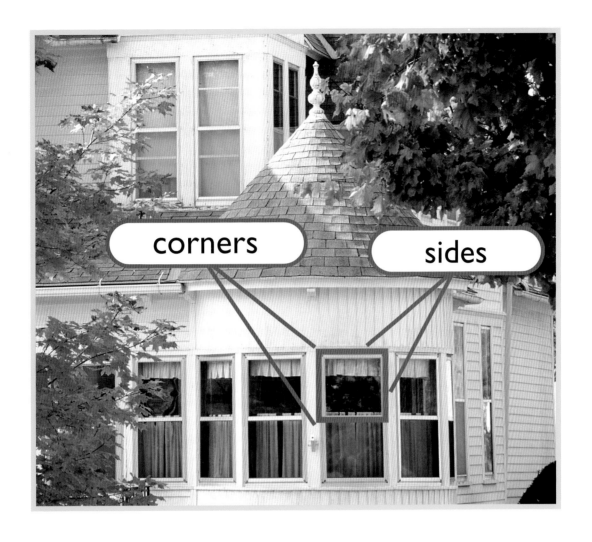

corners

sides

Squares have four corners and four **straight** sides.

All the sides are the same length.

Can I see squares at home?

There are lots of squares at home.

Some of them are in the living room.

Some birthday cards are square.

What other squares can you see
at home?

There are squares in the kitchen.

Some squares are big and some are small.

There are squares in the bathroom.

The square white tiles are smooth and shiny.

Can I see squares at school?

There are lots of squares at school.

You can climb the bars in the gym.

These boards have squares on them.

The squares are red, yellow, blue, and green.

Are there squares in the park?

This playground is in a park.

There are squares on the climbing frame.

Some of the plants in this park are planted in squares.

Different plants are different shades of green.

What do patterns with squares look like?

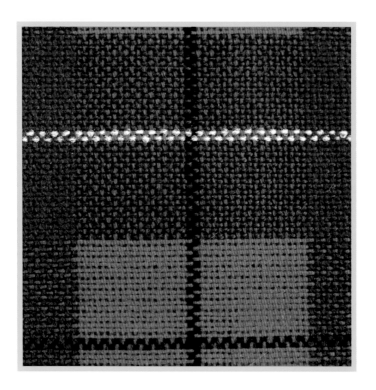

This cloth has a pattern of squares on it.

Cloth like this is used for blankets and rugs.

This board is for playing games.

It has a pattern of blue squares and yellow squares on it.

Can I see squares on other shapes?

faces

You can see squares on a **cube**.

A cube is a **solid** shape with square **faces**.

edges

Cubes have six square faces.

They have **straight edges**.

Are there cubes at school?

These bricks are **cubes**.

You can make a tall tower with them.

Dice are cubes.

They have spots on each **face**.

Can I play games with squares?

You can play noughts and crosses with a friend.

You try to get three in a row.

Each domino has two squares with dots on them.

You can set them up and topple them down.

Can I make squares out of other shapes?

See how many ways you can make squares!

Glossary

cube
shape with six faces that are all the same size

edges
lines where two faces of a shape come together

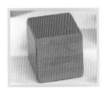
faces
the outside parts of a shape

flat
has no thickness to it

rectangle
flat shape with four straight sides and four corners

solid
has thickness to it, not flat

straight
not bent or curved

Index

Note to parents and teachers

Reading non-fiction texts for information is an important part of a child's literacy development. Readers can be encouraged to ask simple questions and then use the text to find the answers. Each chapter in this book begins with a question. Read the questions together. Look at the pictures. Talk about what the answer might be. Then read the text to find out if your predictions were correct. To develop readers' enquiry skills, encourage them to think of other questions they might ask about the topic. Discuss where you could find the answers. Assist children in using the contents page, picture glossary, and index to practise research skills and new vocabulary.